MW00442161

Contents

Matthew 10:32

"Whosoever therefore shall confess me before men, him will I confess also before my Father which is in heaven."

King James Version

Foreword

The Bible contains many testimonies of people having radical transformations.

- Paul previously killed Christians, had an encounter with God, and then spent the bulk of his life spreading Christianity throughout the region. While in prison, God inspired him to write several profound books which are contained in the Bible. Paul felt inadequate because of his dark past along with a "thorn in the flesh" (2 Corinthians 12:7). However, in 2 Corinthians 12:9, Jesus told Paul, "My grace is sufficient for thee: for my strength is made perfect in weakness." Despite being an imperfect sinner with weaknesses, God used Paul to accomplish great things.

- Moses had a bad reputation for killing someone and felt inadequate in his speech, yet God used him to lead perhaps more than a million Israelites on a forty-year trek from Egypt to modern-day Israel (Exodus 4:10, Numbers 1:46 shows the number of men).

- Noah was ridiculed for acting in faith and building a boat on dry land which people thought was ridiculous. God used Noah to repopulate the earth (Genesis 6-10).

- Job had an extremely challenging life with everything stripped from him. God tested his love, then returned it all back in double (Job 42:10-17).

- David was a scrawny kid with big faith who God empowered to kill a giant with a sling, saving many lives (1 Samuel 17).

- Gideon felt insecure, indecisive and initially wanted to pass on God's calling for him, but God used him to save the nation from oppressors (Judges 6:11-18).

- Peter and John were ordinary "unschooled," uneducated men that God used for big things (Acts 4:13).

Throughout the Bible, God used outcasts, thieves, cheats, lepers, prostitutes, poor, sick, uneducated, highly imperfect people who have made numerous mistakes and failures in life.

God has an affinity for the imperfect, broken, underdogs—ordinary people who feel abnormal and have a hard time feeling "good enough." With God, you are more than good enough. By walking in faith, despite your shortcomings, God turns your weakness into strength and demonstrates His power through you. He loves you and wants you to seek Him.

Introduction

The following testimonies are the stories of real people finding God and positively turning their life around. Each found the strength to overcome difficult challenges- some involving substance abuse, pornography, witchcraft, incarceration, sexual abuse, adultery, and general sin against God. Each person has voluntarily written and submitted their own testimony to share with others in the hope they will be encouraged.

People discover God through unique challenges and transformations. Wherever you are in life's journey, we hope you find these stories relatable, inspiring, and uplifting.

Freedom from Substance Abuse

1 Corinthians 6:20

"For ye are bought with a price: therefore glorify
God in your body, and in your spirit,
which are God's."

King James Version

All Things Work Together for the Good

Audrey Lee Watkins, Detroit, MI, USA

For most of my childhood, I suffered emotional, physical, and sexual abuse.

As the enemy would have it, I began to act out as I got older in all the ways predicted for a person who suffered the kinds of abuses that I suffered. Low self-esteem and self-worth led me to look for and accept love from all the wrong people and places. I can't say that anyone around me had a personal relationship with God, so all that I witnessed were dysfunctional, unhealthy, adulterous, abusive relationships. I began to believe this was the norm.

Also, as predicted, as a young woman, I began to desire escape from my pain, thoughts and memories, and I found that escape (or so I thought) in the form of drugs and alcohol. This led to a period of addiction that spanned for almost thirty years ending with me addicted to crack cocaine and losing everything including my husband and children. Time after time, I tried the Twelve Steps and time after time, I failed in my attempts to stop using drugs. Almost everyone except my beautiful daughter, Nicole, had given up on me.

I kept trying, and my attempts led me to a long-term treatment facility run by the Salvation Army. I tried this once and because of my intellect, I could not receive God as the spiritual help I needed to succeed. I felt like I was smart enough to follow all the steps given me at the program and remain drug-free. I thought I could do it on my own. Little did I know that on my own, I was no match for the devil and his antics.

Six months after I graduated from the facility, I relapsed and began using drugs again. This time, I admitted to myself and God that I couldn't do this alone. I acknowledged that I needed God's help. I asked the administrators at the Salvation Army to come back to the program. They accepted me and my children back into the program, and I made a conscious decision to allow God to take control over my life. In the meantime, my daughter Nicole had gotten saved and started to share her salvation experiences with me.

On December 22, 1999, I received Jesus Christ as my Lord and Savior and began my journey toward God's perfect will for my life. Thirteen years later, I became an Evangelist with an MBA. I am an Addictions Counselor, and I teach Addiction Recovery at my local ministry. By the grace of God, I am good at my job because of all the things that I suffered.

Today, I truly know that all things work together for good to them that love God and to them that are the called according to His purpose.

A New Freedom

Mike Nicholas, Springfield, TN, USA

My name is Mike Nicholas. I grew up in a broken home. I was forced to live with many people, including grandparents, uncles, aunts, church members, and whomever else they could pawn me off on.

I knew who God was at an early stage in my life; I was forced to go to church every time the doors were open. I didn't believe in Jesus because I could not touch Him or see Him.

At an early age in my life, I was introduced to sex, drugs, and alcohol. You name it—if it was bad for me, I knew about it.

I married my wife, Staci, at the age of seventeen and was consumed still with drugs and alcohol. We were far away from the church. We now have three daughters: Ashley, Brittany, and Loren, who I also kept from the church except for rare occasions when I would go, or they attended with friends.

The alcohol consumed me. I still worked hard every day but drank from the time I got off work until bedtime. Sometimes I just would pass out somewhere, and they would leave me there.

I have done a ton of damage over twenty-three years of my marriage. I was never physically abusive to my wife or daughters. But they were always afraid I would hit them. I was verbally abusive and would cuss them right out.

My wife kicked me out of the house in October 2012 for hurting her for the last time. She was hurt and stunned as were my kids and entire family for the terrible things I had done. I had ripped this family apart.

There I was, all alone in a motel room trying to figure out what I had done. I opened the drawer to the nightstand, and I saw a Bible, opened it up, and started reading. I stayed in that room for six days, just God and me. All day, all night.

I asked God to forgive me and come into my heart and save me from my alcohol addiction—to take it completely out of my mind. I cried so much in that room calling up to Him, begging Him, "Lord Jesus, Please, Please don't let me lose my family. If you do this for me, I will serve you for the rest of my life." I haven't had a drink since October 17, 2012. No help, just me and God (praise Jesus). John 14:14, "If you ask anything in my name, I will do it." God said it, and I believed it.

After this miracle from God, I returned home with forgiveness from my family. I told them I was a changed man and I was going to live my life for Jesus. We started a church here at the Life Center the last week of December 2012. And now, all three of my daughters have received Jesus as their Lord and Savior and all three baptized and living by the words of God. Praise Jesus!

From The Fog, into the Light, Overnight

Sean, Mabank, TX, USA

I was raised in a good family setting as a kid, but never really knew how to connect with God. My parents took me to church a few times, but I really never did grasp the whole concept.

By the time I was fifteen, I had started drinking and smoking marijuana with no direction or plan for my future. I continued to smoke marijuana at least five to ten times a day for the next eight years. I used to feel like I had no purpose in life and kept hitting dead end after dead end. I became very depressed inside without even realizing it. I would turn to getting high to deal with every situation I came across.

At the age of twenty-two, I discovered marijuana concentrates, a very potent form of marijuana which kept me very consumed and distracted from any chance of touching base with reality. I would come home from work and spend the rest of my day getting high and avoiding my family and people. I lived a very selfish lifestyle and lived only to get high.

At the age of twenty-four, I had worked several different jobs; each were dead ends. I had become very depressed and broke, not a dollar in my pocket, and no food in the fridge. It was that day I finally hit rock bottom and broke down in tears, realizing I had been off path for too many years and I knew it wasn't right.

That night, I reached out to God in tears, I prayed and begged for forgiveness of my selfish life full of sin, I asked God to release me from the sins that had me bound. I prayed for work and another chance at life, and it was at that very moment I could feel my anxiety and fears lifting from my body, my mind lit up like never before, I could feel the connection. He was there with me. It was the first time in my life that I had actually prayed and I felt it. My heart was crying out for God's wisdom and guidance.

I woke up the next morning at 7 AM to a phone call from my old boss telling me he had plenty of work for me and to get ready to stay busy. I jumped out of bed with an indescribable force of energy and motivation. My life was bright and full of joy because I knew I had finally made a real change and it happened only through God's will. Overnight, I turned my back on marijuana and never looked back. It wasn't as if I quit; I just shed the addiction like a winter coat. I was simply no longer interested in getting high. He helped me change my entire perspective literally overnight.

It's been three weeks now; I haven't had the slightest urge to return to my old lifestyle. I look back at my old self, and it brings me to tears to see how lost and desperate I once was. It was only three weeks ago, but it feels like ten years.

I have honestly been reborn. I am truly high on life. I read the Bible every chance I get and pray three or four times a day. It's amazing how far I've come in this short amount of time. It is honestly a miracle I haven't ended up in prison for all of my poor decisions.

God has always been here watching over me, all it took was one full-hearted prayer to open the door to fill that empty void in my heart. God truly healed my weeping soul overnight. Now, I spend my days praising the Lord and spreading the message to my family and close friends. I feel ashamed that it has taken me twenty-four years to finally see the light and get on the right path.

My life has never been full of love and kindness, just like the Bible says. I soar like an eagle with wings; my days are no longer a struggle. I wake up every morning and thank the Lord for allowing me just one more day to get closer to Him and praise His amazing works. I could type for days in detail about how He has filled me with wisdom and positive energy, but I will stop here to say a prayer for us all; we all deserve to see the light.

I Went From Selling "Dope" to Selling "Hope"

Brother Frank, Norwalk, CT, USA

Before I chose to walk with God, I idolized other people and worldly possessions. I needed to feel in control. I needed to feel powerful in others' eyes. I made awful decisions through this lonely and destructive period of my life. I chose to run with a dangerous crowd and sell drugs.

Sadly, I believed at that time that I was a success. I drove beautiful cars: Mercedes, BMW, Corvettes, had beautiful girlfriends, whatever clothes or materials I wanted and money in my pockets. I had so much money at one point I had to start hiding it under my mattress. I thought this would bring me all the happiness and fulfillment I could ever want. I was so wrong. It was never enough.

My soul was spiritually bankrupt. I did not trust anyone. I lived in fear and paranoia daily. I did not treat others well including my parents and the people in my life I was supposed to care about. I was selfish and self-destructive. I steamrolled over others to get my way and needs met. There's a saying, 'He sold his soul to the devil.' I completely relate to it.

Regardless of all the money I had and all the so-called influential people and connections I knew, I was empty inside. I turned to drugs and alcohol to numb my pain. Cocaine was my drug of choice and Jack Daniels my drink of choice. The high felt wonderful at the time, and the lows were so low that I could not look at myself in the mirror the next day. I was on a chaotic evil, destructive cycle, and I was dragging everyone around that loved me down with me. The tears and sleepless nights I caused my loved ones did not matter because my life was only about me. I was arrested for my drug dealing and spent a few years in prison. I was still so misguided that I blamed everyone else. The police, the state attorney, they were all out to get me. I got out of jail and spent years blaming others and hurting others due to my selfishness and lack of Christ in my life.

I was born and raised Catholic, and I believed in Jesus, but I never understood what it was to have a true relationship with Him. My first step in connecting with Jesus was through a Christian television show. I saw Joel Osteen on television and was intrigued by his positive messages and his faith and belief in Jesus. Still, deep down inside, I felt this relationship was what God meant for others, not me. I was such a sinner and had made so many bad decisions in my life; there was no way God would want this same relationship with me. This past spring, I decided to go to church with a friend. Honestly, I believed I did it to stop the nagging. I figured I would go once and get it over with. After all, I was already close to Jesus, or so I thought. We walked into the church, and that sermon was the beginning of my true walk with Christ. The pastor was telling us his life history. He had been in trouble with the law when he was younger. I understood then that God was reaching out to me yet again and genuinely loved me even with all my sins. I felt such a peace come over me. It was surreal. This was a pure and beautiful peace. I felt hope and love. This marked the beginning of my true journey to walk with Christ.

I know now Jesus has always been with me. It was I that turned my back on Him. I used to run away from Jesus, and now I run as fast as I can towards Him. It was I that chose evil ways. Jesus was always waiting for me with open arms to choose Him instead. I am blessed to walk with Jesus now. This love, peace, and understanding fill my heart every day. The Bible is the most important material in my life now. My relationship with Jesus is far more important than any other in this world. Since I have chosen to walk with Jesus, I am now healing from so many past negative decisions. I am prospering in His love and His word. Past relationships I thought could never be mended are now being repaired. Behaviors I felt I could never change does. There is such a spiritual peace and well-being in my life it beats out the most expensive Mercedes or Air Jordan's any day. Jesus has performed a miracle in my life, and I thank Him every day.

I know now my true purpose in life is to bring my experiences to others that have or faced similar struggles and to guide them to Jesus' love and protection. It is my mission to help others find that true relationship and walk in Jesus' name. I am looking forward to volunteering in The Prison Fellowship in order to share God's word.

God Bless, and remember: Jesus is waiting for you. He loves you and is ready to work miracles in your life as well. Open your heart to Him. For me, it is not an opportunity to serve God; it is an obligation.

Blessings,
Brother Frank

Never Alone

Jenny

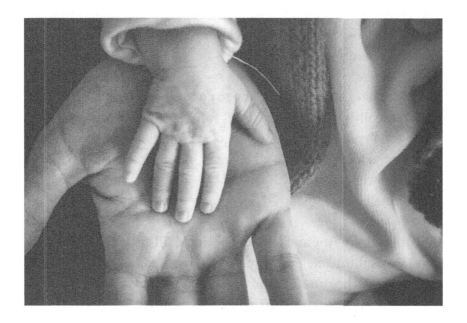

I was brought up in church and went every Sunday morning, Sunday night, and Wednesdays up until my mother got sick when I was twenty-eight. I went because I had to, but believed Jesus was real. I wanted what my mother and older sister had: peace, even though life is crazy.

That pretty much stopped after my brother and two other sisters found out our mother was dying of cancer. We had three weeks to say goodbye, and during that time, our mother continued to be strong in the Lord, praising His name time and time again. This meant nothing to me at the time. I just knew my "momma" was dying, and I couldn't do anything to help her.

She died in 2002 and my younger sister and I went wild. Drinking, partying, all the stuff our dear mother tried to keep us from. But during all my wasting of time, I would always have the thought that I shouldn't be here. I shouldn't be doing this or that. I would drown out those thoughts as quickly as I could with whatever alcohol I was drinking at the time.

My older sister started asking me to go to church with her, and I couldn't really give her an excuse. I would wait until the evening service so I could get over my hangover from the night before. I even went a few times with a hangover, but I went with her. And as I sat in church listening, I learned I was a sinner going to a sinner's hell.

God opened my eyes and let me see what a filthy person I was and that I was splitting hell wide open. God sent an evangelist my way. This man also became a friend over time, and God used him to also help me see that I wasn't saved and right with the Lord.

One night in July of 2005, the Lord convicted me and brought me to my knees. I cried out to Him to save this wretched soul that is a sinner who needs a Savior! I thank my Lord Jesus for hearing and answering my cry.

I look back over the years and now can say that I was never alone. Not once during all those times when I felt so very alone and scared and useless. God used my mother, my sister, leading me to church and also my evangelist friend.

It has not been easy. Sometimes, I still get the urge to drink, and I ask the Lord to help with my temptation. It's not all sunny smiles and roses, but I trust my Lord and Savior to help, to lead, and guide me. He is my hope and my life. To Jesus, I give all the glory and praise! He saved me, and I thank His blessed name! And I continue to pray that God will open my younger sister's eyes and she will turn to Him soon.

Alcohol to El-Shaddai (The Lord Almighty)

Malvin Raj, Kuala Lumpur, Malaysia

I was seventeen when I started to drink. You know, teenage life/party/functions will never go on without alcohol. I used to get high easily when I started. Then I began to compete with my friends to drink more than them. The alcoholic spirit began to control me. I became so addicted to alcohol I couldn't go on a day without it.

People used to drink and compete with me. I bought juice bottles, poured them out, and filled them with beers to bring it to my workplace. I used to drink in public trains, theaters, shopping malls, roadsides, and even consuming alcohol before taking the Holy Communion.

Then one day, I came across this verse: Proverbs 20:1, "Drinking too much makes you loud and foolish. It is stupid to get drunk." This verse slapped me hard. I found it interesting, and I wanted to know more about what the Bible says about drinking. Ephesians 5:8 says, "Do not get drunk with wine, which will only ruin you; instead, be filled with the Spirit." This verse made me realize that alcohol was only ruining me all this while. So I wondered, what Spirit is that verse saying I need to be filled with it. I started to read the Bible. So John 8:32 says, "Know the truth, then the truth will set you free."

Then I knew it. The truth is the Bible. The Bible is the Word of God. The Word of God is Jesus Himself as John 1:1 says: "In the beginning was the WORD, the WORD was with GOD, and the WORD is GOD!"

Amen, Hallelujah! God has changed my life seriously; He's EL-SHADDAI, God Almighty. Almighty, as in, He can do wonders in anyone's life. It's just us; we need to realize His touch, His Words, and His Grace. If Jesus can change me, then there's no doubt Jesus can change you too.

Praise the Lord! JESUS LOVES YOU :)

Broken

Anonymous

I was saved in 1980. I had been living a life that had worn me out, and I wasn't even twenty-one years old yet.

Working in a mill at night, a truck driver didn't see me and leveled his load of logs by rolling one off the top, and it landed on my foot. It was like a slow-motion event, and then it hit my foot. In that moment, I noticed an awareness was about me, and I knew an angel was with me, and the log, which was an inch from my face, went flying hard, far away from me. Around that time, a sense of calmness washed over me, and I kept my head telling those panicking around me what to do to help me. The Lord was with me, and apparently, I didn't need that part of my foot because I lost it.

I was pregnant out of wedlock at the time. Being a single parent was challenging, and having an atheist as the father of my child complicated my life significantly.

It cannot be stressed enough, being a new Christian and a single parent, the challenges faced, and acceptance in churches and society are the biggest.

My family was not supportive. I was alone. Even the people in my church, never reached out to me even when I asked for help, not money, but friendship would have been enough. It never happened. I had no friends even after reaching out many times. I went there for four years. I studied the Word intensely for several years, and later would be very glad I did. Having no support system, I became a vulnerable prey. A mentally sick man, who lived in the apartment on the other side of us, harassed me every single day for two years. I was stalked by my daughter's dad, assisted by my own family, and I lost custody of my daughter because nobody could understand why I was struggling. They were all married, had families, and strong support systems.

After years of fighting for my daughter and me, I lost everything to money because my daughter's dad had a mother who married a wealthy man, and they wanted her. I lost custody after my two sisters lied in court because they hated me and our entire lives. I was abandoned by all I thought should care for me. I was struggling with my faith because all I had believed was at its stress point. I backslid at this point. I drank, not a lot, but enough, and lost who I was. I had people in my life who were violent, and alcoholic. Yet, I still felt the Lord there.

After ten years of grieving over the loss of my daughter and my life, I finally came to myself and had regained my faith. Though I was hurting, I began to realize God allowed me to go through this so He would be the foundation of my life, and not anyone else. This gave me strength, and whenever I have felt my faith weakening, the Lord would undergird me with His faith. I still have a difficult family, and sadly, my daughter's dad, who took his own life several months ago, and my daughter, who is struggling with all the misinformation she was told about me for so long, and she is suffering depression. We are still reconciling, though we have some very rough days.

I still have days when my faith is tested. So many years have worn me down, and I am quite tired. However, the Lord is faithful, and always present to encourage me when I struggle. It has been since 1991 that I have been restored to the Lord, and I can honestly say today that He is my fortress, and I look to Him, who is always present. "When your father and mother leave you, then the Lord will take you up" — this verse has been proved in my life a lot, and I know God loves me. I know whose I am, and who I am. Now, I am at another crossroads, as I just lost a sister to cancer, another sister has been battling cancer for several years, and my mom just finished chemo. Yet, I feel God calling me away from here, to go somewhere else, and it is difficult because though it is a challenge, and I am somewhat scared to go, that is what I believe the Father is leading me to do.

The point of my testimony is to persevere, and not give up. If you fall, He will be there to lift you up again. His love and consistency are dependable, and He provides all I need. Forgiveness is worth learning, and we are never to stop growing in our faith.

Freedom from False Teachings

John 14:6

"Jesus saith unto him, I am the way, the truth, and the life: no man cometh unto the Father, but by me."

King James Version

From Satan to Christ

Doug Buchanan, Casper, Wyoming, USA

I was raised Mormon in an abusive household. It seemed boring and lifeless to me, and I couldn't respect a religion my abusive father belonged to. Growing up, I had emotional, behavioral, and developmental problems. Among them: Asperger's Syndrome, bipolar disorder, borderline personality disorder, and PTSD as a result of the abuse. In addition, I had a low immune system and chronic migraines.

When I was thirteen, in a search for power and personal development, I began experimenting with the occult and Satanism. After I was freed from a possession, I turned to Wicca, which I saw as lighter and safer and filled with love, which I now realize to be a lie and a disguise. When I was sixteen, I came out to my parents as bisexual. My parents kicked me out of the house when I was nineteen, in the beginning of December. I remember being heartbroken and scared, thinking I was going to die alone on the street. I managed to get a hotel room for a few nights before catching a bus to Idaho to live with a friend. Her landlord kicked me out after two weeks as I was not on the lease.

From there, I went to a homeless shelter and saved up enough money to go to Casper, Wyoming, to be with my long-distance girlfriend of one and a half years where there is a Christian Rescue Mission for homeless people. I was scared they would try to convert me. They didn't. I lived there for three months. Near the end of the first month, my then girlfriend cheated on me. I fell into a major depressive state. I was walking at night, and my left foot was run over by a pickup. I went to the hospital and got x-rays. I was blessed (though at the time, in my ignorance, I attributed it to the Wiccan goddess rather than the true God), as there was not even a hairline fracture. I was in a walking boot and crutches for two weeks. At the library, a nice Christian lady asked to pray for me to recover from my injury quickly, and I accepted. The next morning, I did not need the boot or crutches. Still, I denied Christ.

One day, I felt a need to go to the library and go to the second floor. While there, I met a Christian (not Mormon) girl, Danae, whose plans to travel to Texas that week had been canceled due to unforeseen difficulties. We now believe God planned that. We quickly became friends and started dating shortly after. I asked to attend her church's youth group with her, merely to spend more time with her. Then I went to church with her that Sunday.

At my second youth group with her, I felt something stirring in me. During my third session, I felt the urge to tear off my pentacle necklace. After that youth group, as she was taking me back to the Mission, I asked her to pull over in a secluded area so we could talk about youth group. She agreed. I shared with her my feelings and told her about a dream I had had the previous night which seemed to suggest I would convert. We prayed. I pulled out my pocket knife and cut the string to my pentacle necklace, throwing the pendant across the street and as far away from me as I could.

That week, at church, Pastor was praying and said, "And God, please bless the person in this room who has been dabbling in witchcraft. Release him from his bonds." Nobody in the church besides Danae, her mom, and our friend (Noel) knew about my history of witchcraft. I felt God's spirit in me then.

After church, Pastor sent out his weekly newsletter to members of the ministry, which included Danae's mom. She told me part of the newsletter, which detailed how Pastor had felt God telling him as he prayed to pray for the one dabbling in witchcraft. He thought it was strange at first, but knew he had to obey God. My passion for God had ignited suddenly and powerfully. I obtained a Bible and a cross necklace and strove to learn everything I could about God and the Gospel. Over the next few weeks, I attended church and youth group every week. I asked God into my heart multiple times as I felt like I needed to show God how passionate I was about Him.

Finally, only two short weeks ago, I was baptized. It was the most beautiful experience of my life, even if the water was freezing! I had been baptized when I was eight, like any Mormon child, but as I didn't choose to do it on my own and as I had left Christ completely, I felt like it was important to do it on my own. I just turned twenty only three days ago.

My journey to Christ has happened fast and has been entirely life-changing. I am no longer homeless, and I no longer struggle with depression or homosexuality of any form. Danae and I are still going strong, and the only one I love more than Danae is God. I thank God every night in my heart for bringing Danae into my life and using her to bring me to Him. God bless you all. I love you all.

When the Good News Reached Me

Anonymous

I am a forty-three-year-old Indian homemaker who lives in Indonesia. I was born into a Hindu family and had never questioned my religion. I followed whatever had to be done as a Hindu. For me, this meant lighting a lamp in the evening at 6 pm and visiting a temple when I made my annual visit to India. It meant celebrating certain festivals and praying to idols and pictures of Hindu gods at home.

I didn't have a very difficult life but was certainly in the dark about many things. I was highly opinionated and quick to argue and debate on every topic under the sun. I had constant mood swings where I could spend a moment on cloud nine and then go down deep into the dumps, depending on my situation. But most of all,

I was a constant worrier. There was this hole inside of me that I tried to satisfy with socializing and eating.

Things changed when I placed my child in a Christian school. The school was strong in its sharing of Biblical verses, and as the warm and comfortable atmosphere that the teachers provided grew on me, I began to notice the opening and closing prayers at assemblies or other such gatherings.

The Bible verses used as themes for the year opened my eyes to Christian behavior, and many of the teachers were practicing them which also touched my heart. I remember at one Christmas assembly when a teacher gave a message which said: *Jesus was the only way to heaven.* I felt upset and complained about this to the principal. When the teacher was confronted with this, he and his wife began praying for me.

Meanwhile, I had formed a good friendship with the teacher's wife who I felt was one of the nicest persons I had ever met. She began a Bible study group, and I joined.

I began to love the teachings and most of all, I started to fall in love with Jesus. To me, Jesus seemed perfect, holy, and without sin. I knew this through the many messages the school was sharing, but I believe the Holy Spirit was working on my heart with these thoughts. One day, I declared to a group of teachers at the school that I loved Christianity, but couldn't do anything about it because I was born Hindu. God must have had a good hearty laugh at that!

A few months later, I saw a link online that said there was evidence that Jesus was God. I clicked it and was stunned at the deep and clear research that had been done. But it was a picture of a Jesus in the background whose eyes seemed to be piercing my soul that made me realize what a sinner I was. Suddenly, I saw all my sins in front of my eyes. I saw the cross with Jesus on it, and I saw the truth. Jesus was the only God.

He had died for me. I was a sinner. Only His blood would clean me and open the gates to heaven. I just had to believe in this and receive Him.

It took me a week to decide what to do. I feared the Hindu gods would punish me. But one night, I got the answer: "When God is with you, who can be against you?" I received Jesus. My life was never the same after that. No longer did I worry. No longer was I empty. The hole was filled with Jesus.

I walked in the light, clearly knowing what was wrong and what was right as the Bible verses and the Holy Spirit showed me many things. I began to love people as I saw them through Jesus' eyes. He brought financial blessings like never before. He gave me strength when I was diagnosed with a benign tumor. Jesus gave me peace and joy. The good news had given me freedom.

Experience of a True Love of Jesus by a Hindu Brahmin Girl

Mamatha, Bangalore, Karnataka, India

I was born and raised in a Hindu Brahmin's family. My family is very orthodox. I was a true follower and believer of idols and statues as my parents showed me a photo of Ishwar and Parvathi from when I was born. I believed they are real and the true God until my graduation. I thought they are the real God.

During my graduation, I met one of my classmates who was a Christian RC. After meeting her every day, I became close to her, and I was interested to know about Jesus, so I kept asking her every day. I hadn't even heard of the Bible back then. After that, unknowingly, I started to believe in Jesus. One day, I asked my friend if Jesus is also God like our Hindu gods.

One day, I went to her residence to study. Her brother was watching a movie about the Ten Commandments. I was sitting on a sofa, waiting for my friend. All of a sudden, my eyes moved to watch that movie, *Ten Commandments*, when Moses went to bring the Ten Commandments from God. Aaron made a bull and told everyone this is the God who saved all from the Egyptians. After that, some people went with Moses, and some were separated from Him and started believing that bull is God. Then my heart felt that Jesus is the true God. From then onwards, I started believing in only Jesus Christ. I have accepted Jesus into my heart as my Savior and that through Him, I can gain eternal life (the year 2002).

After nine years (2011), I was praying to Jesus like I had prayed to Hindu idols and deities. I didn't even know Bible verses or the Word of God. Like this, I lived, accepting Jesus without knowing any of His Words. Later I started my career, but yet to get married, as my family—parents and brothers started hating me for being a believer of Jesus Christ. Every day, my family scolded me. Everyone in my family hated me. One day, I was very sad and about to leave home and commit suicide, and then I met a preacher of God. He prayed for me for two hours over the phone and told me to meditate on the words, *Jesus I love you*. I did as instructed.

After meditating, the word of God filled me with His love. It's an unconditional love I never experienced in my life. It was a fantastic experience of the true love of Jesus. I had no words to express Jesus' love, (John 21:17), Jesus asked Peter, "Do you love me?" The first time, Peter said, "Yes, Lord, I love you." Again, Jesus asked Peter, "Do you love me?" Then he said, "Yes, Lord, I love you." At last, a third time, Jesus asked Peter, "Do you really love me? Then Peter cried and told Jesus, "Lord, you know everything. You know that I love you." Like this verse, I started to cry until the Lord filled me with His love.

(The year 2011) I came to know about the word of God, i.e., Bible. I heard reading this will make me close to Jesus, and He will talk to us through His Word. Matthew 6:33 says, "But seek ye first the kingdom of God and his righteousness, and all these things shall be added unto you." After I started reading the Bible and going to church every day, God gradually changed my life, filled everywhere with His love. He made my enemies my friends. In 2013, God blessed me with my life partner. Now, I am living my life happy with the presence of Jesus.

The Word of God changed my life. Luke 21:33 says, *"Heaven and earth shall pass away: but my words shall not pass away."*

I kindly request everyone to pray for my family and everyone in this world who is not aware of the truth about Jesus; that God should open their heart and fill them with His wisdom so that they might understand the love of Jesus and accept Him.

God makes a way where it seems to be no way.

Accepting Christ

Lori, Gaines, MI, USA

What would it take for you to accept Christ when you have rejected Him so many times? What would it take for you to be transformed from lost to found in Jesus Christ? Would it take a lot? It certainly did in my case.

When I think of my journey so far, I know that He transformed me and made me new. You see, I was not raised in a Christian home and had no Christians in my world to lead by example. I was a very lost young woman, but praise be to God, He brought me into His kingdom.

You may think, 'Yeah, right. What's she been smoking?' I realize that it sounds crazy to the world, but this is my testimony:

My parents divorced when I was seven. My mom raised my sister and I the best she could, but she was a single parent and worked full time just trying to pay the bills. My dad left the state, and we didn't hear from him again for twenty-one years. We were often on welfare and moved from place to place as we got behind on the rent. It was not a great childhood. I started smoking pot at the age of thirteen.

By fifteen, I was doing drugs and drinking. At the same age, I started getting involved in witchcraft, casting spells, playing around with an Ouija board and basically anything involved with witchcraft. By the age of seventeen, I started getting involved in New Age, reincarnation, crystals, and all that goes with it. Drugs and drinking remained a theme throughout my youth, also. By the age of twenty-one, I was teaching New Age classes and was heavily into both New Age and drinking/drugs.

Why do I tell you all these? Because you have to understand where I was and my attitude at this time. I really hated Christians. I had an attitude that said, 'Who are they to judge me and cram their morality down my throat?' I would often curse Christians. I had a couple of friends in high school witness to me, but I rejected their attempts. In truth, I now know my problem was not with Christians, but with God. God made the standards He wants us to live by, not Christians. But at this point, I was all about rebellion, wickedness, and sin.

At age twenty-one, I married an alcoholic man and was married to him for the next sixteen years. We continued in what drew us together—drinking, drugs, and witchcraft. After divorcing him, I began seeking some kind of peace in my life. I met and married my current husband who was what I would call a nominal Christian. I started to see that He had the peace I was seeking.

I started thinking, 'What is the big deal with Jesus, anyway?' I became curious and picked up a couple of books (not a Bible) about Him. Shortly after seeking Jesus, He appeared to me in a vision.

I saw Him as a skeletal, emaciated man wearing a white robe that was glowing from within. I felt I had to reach out and touch the hem of His robe. (I didn't know this was scriptural as I had never even touched a Bible). I reached out to touch Him and heard voices (the enemy) saying, 'No! Don't touch Him. You will hurt Him. No! Stop!' I knew it was something I must do and I had to touch His robe.

When I touched His sleeve, He was transformed into a healthy, strong man but the transformation was not about Him, I was the one transformed! He looked me squarely in the eye and said, "In your past, you have had no time for me. Now, all that has changed for me." When I looked into His eyes, I knew there was nothing I could hide. He saw everything about me including my mountains of sin and my wickedness. I looked into His eyes and saw such incredible love! I felt such love I had never felt before. But there was not just love, but mercy, justice, peace, and judgment.

Nobody in this world wants to talk about judgment, but it is there, too. Also holiness! I felt that I was shot through with a million volts of electricity. It is difficult to describe what I felt in earthly words as there is nothing of this world that can describe all that

He is. When I realized who He was, I could stand in His presence no longer and fell on my face before Him. I not only fell on my face but began pleading, *mercy, mercy, Lord!*

Then I started speaking in a language I had never heard. The words poured out of my mouth. I didn't know what it was but realized it was in praise to Him as I lay on my face before Jesus. The next thing I knew, He was gone. I was still speaking in tongues. Tears were streaming down my face. I still felt like electricity was flowing through me as His Holy presence left me. (I realized later I had received forgiveness and the infilling of the Holy Spirit when I began attending church and reading my Bible).

That happened seventeen years ago, and as I recall all that happened that day and type this, I am crying. He is so real! If you don't know Him, but would like to, I would say sincerely seek Him.

Ask, search, seek. He is looking for a sincere heart and wants to make His home in you and transform your life. I was on my way to the devil's hell and had rejected Him, but in His mercy and grace, He brought me out of that and wrote my name in His Lamb's Book of Life.

Today, my husband and I have been married twenty years. We attend church together and often volunteer, pray, and study together. I feel very blessed to have such a Godly man as a husband.

Maybe as you read this, you are thinking, 'This lady is looney.' Perhaps I am, but this is my testimony, and I know in my heart of hearts, Jesus is the Truth. Again, I would ask you, what would it take to change your life, and transform your mind?

Some have asked me if I think I'm somebody special because He appeared to me. The answer is no! I am a dust mote on the sea of humanity, but God in His mercy reached down and made me His daughter by the precious blood of His only begotten Son, Jesus Christ. I am eternally grateful to Jesus, and I am forever changed. Praise God!

I leave you with one of my favorite scriptures:

"For the word of God is quick, and powerful, and sharper than any twoedged sword, piercing even to the dividing asunder of soul and spirit, and of the joints and marrow, and is a discerner of the thoughts and intents of the heart." Hebrews 4:12 KJV

If you seek Jesus, read the Bible, particularly read the New Testament and ask Him into your heart to forgive you of your sins and have Him be the Lord of your life. You will be forever changed!

"And Jesus said unto them, I am the bread of life: he that cometh to me shall never hunger; and he that believeth on me shall never thirst." John 6:35 KJV

A New Creature

Jessica, Lebanon, NJ, USA

Before Jesus saved me, I was steeped in and infatuated for most of my teenage years with pornography, writing and reading explicit sexual stories on the internet, as well as not being celibate with my then boyfriend. I also had an addiction to sexual fantasies and sexual acts. After Jesus saved me with His Word, I am now not at all interested, nor do I watch, read, or write sexual material.

Before Jesus saved me, I was haunted by childhood memories of sexual abuse (both as a victim and even perpetrator, experimenting with others). After Jesus saved me, I forgave everyone and also asked for forgiveness, and also, I am extremely happy nor do I give thought to those thoughts brought up by Satan to remind me.

Before Jesus saved me, I was participating, both knowingly and unknowingly, in witchcraft, New Age, and eastern spiritual activities. I was continuously tormented day and night by demons who actually abused me physically, mentally, emotionally, spiritually, and sexually. I was at the point of suicide. After Jesus saved me, I have had peaceful nights' sleep because He blankets me in His mercy, grace, hope, and love.

Before Jesus saved me, I was slothful, lying in bed all day after work (if I didn't call out) or school until I would get sore and weak all over. Even worse, on days off, I would literally go the whole day without getting up or eating barely anything, not even showering. My bed was my prison.

After Jesus saved me, I must always move, and I'm excited about life and my goals, dreams, interests, and what God is doing. Oh, and I love to shower!

Before Jesus saved me, I had no one to talk to. Literally no one. I lost contact with all friends because I never talked, nor did I want to get out of bed or the house to go anywhere. A few times I was alone at home on Christmas, not caring, yet deep down crying to be with others. I even ignored family.

After Jesus saved me, He has put me in contact with many loving people at my church, a lot my age, and also I hang out with my family every chance I get. Furthermore, God is the most desirable friend I have ever had. I am completely satisfied with His goodness, love, and purity, and His character and personality. He is my best friend, the first one I had once I was saved. He was there when no one else was there.

Before Jesus saved me, I was moving down the road to becoming a full-blown homosexual. I was bisexual, and had interest in women, and hated men with a passion and was scared of them, even of them looking at me. I wrote homosexual stories, watched homosexual pornography, and was even ready to sign up on a website that catered to individuals who wanted to date in this lifestyle.

After Jesus saved me, within the same week, these homosexual thoughts and feelings felt very foreign to my body. It felt as if these emotions and feelings were being sent to my body from Satan and his demons, and these feelings were in opposition to my natural body's gender. With the Holy Spirit in me, and me agreeing with Him that these feelings were not mine and were from Satan, God blocked the feelings, and I actually began to like guys again. I began to lose interest in women, and now I don't have it at all nor do I want it.

I accepted Christ by being convicted of my sins after watching a series of YouTube videos. Then I went to my mom for help in getting out of darkness, and she led me in the salvation prayer. It was a very long rocky road of learning, growing, and chastisement since then, but, I would not trade it for the world because of the close relationship with God that I have. I consider Him my best friend and cannot imagine a life without Him.

I am so blessed to know God as a friend. I have been through a few challenging trials, medically, emotionally, and spiritually, but God was and continues to be by my side every step of the way. He healed me from many deceptive spiritual practices and beliefs also.

I got married a year and a half ago to a very wonderful, strong Christian man who helps grow me in Christ and go to a strong Biblical church. I cannot imagine a day going by without dwelling on my God, pondering His faithfulness, greatness, and holiness, and cannot imagine a day going by without sowing into our friendship by reading the Bible and talking/praying to Him.
I love God so much.

Jesus and His truth, His light, and His precious gift to me, the gift being He died on the cross for every single sin I have ever committed, and then rising the third day to completely defeat Satan and his demons and all of sin and death's power. He has set me free and given me every promise in His Holy Word, the Bible.

"Therefore if any man be in Christ, he is a new creature: old things are passed away; behold, all things are become new."
2 Corinthians 5:17 KJV

Freedom from Pornography

1 John 2:16-17

"For all that is in the world, the lust of the flesh, and the lust of the eyes, and the pride of life, is not of the Father, but is of the world. And the world passeth away, and the lust thereof: but he that doeth the will of God abideth for ever."

King James Version

From Adultery to Victory in Christ Jesus

Desmond Geduldt, Cape Town, South Africa

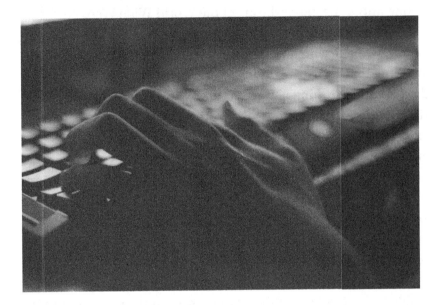

I remember when I was much younger, having grown up on the cape flats, being surrounded by gangsters, drugs, and alcohol, saying to myself that I would never allow an addiction to get the better of me because I was in complete control of my life (or so I thought!). At the age of fourteen, I developed a love for computers, and at age fifteen, I hacked into the school's mainframe computer and downloaded exam papers way ahead of the exams.

At the age of sixteen, I was made chairperson of the school's computer club as well as an organization called CICS. Today, I am a qualified I.T. Specialist, an achievement most computer technicians only dream of. Am I proud of my accomplishment? To be honest with you, I don't even know how to answer that question. In 1996, internet became popular in South Africa, and my love for computers grew even stronger. I soon came to learn that the Internet gave a person access to anything from the study of DNA to downloading music to mention but a few. It was not long until I mastered the art of the World Wide Web.

One day, while researching on the internet, I stumbled across something that really caught my attention—it was a video clip of a naked woman touching herself. At first, I was a bit embarrassed, but that didn't stop me from visiting that same website again and again. Was that an addiction surfacing? Not according to my standards. Soon, internet cafes started blocking sites containing pornographic material by putting up firewalls, but that didn't stop me from accessing these websites. My expertise allowed me to break through their firewalls and security systems. I didn't realize it at the time, but my willpower was driven by a strong demonic force called a spirit of lust.

I couldn't stop thinking of the images I saw on the internet. In fact, I became so addicted to pornography that I used any excuse to get away from my home just to go to an internet cafe to look at pornographic material. I remember telling my wife at one stage that I got a six-month contract to maintain the network of an internet cafe and it required of me to work during the nights. I never worked at the internet cafes; I just went there at nights to look at pornographic material and to meet girls online. I was so excited when I got my own modem for my computer as it meant I could browse the internet in the comfort of my own home.

My addiction grew stronger and stronger. I started giving up my sleep for the Internet. By the time my eldest son was born, I developed a nasty habit of chatting up women on late at nights, asking them to send me naked pictures of themselves. I would use these images to fantasize and please myself in front of my computer.

Pornography started controlling my life and the more the internet expanded; the more my addiction to pornography grew. I recall how excited I was when the webcam was invented, making it now possible to bring a woman from anywhere in the world right into the comfort of your own bedroom.

I started living a double life, and because of my addiction, it became costly. I was forced to use my I.T. skills to defraud business owners, airline companies, and hotels, not to mention the damage this caused to families. Hacking was child's play for me, and I used computer software to generate credit card details then I would order hi-tech equipment online, as well as book airline tickets and then sell them for next to nothing. I would furthermore use the credit card details to book into 5-star hotels and also rent vehicles from car rental companies; then I would have the vehicles trackers removed and sell the cars valued at over $7,000 for as little as $200, sometimes even less depending on how badly I needed cash.

In early 2000, I made headlines in the major newspapers by being the first technician to advertise a business of unblocking blacklisted, or rather stolen, cell phones, as well as removing the security codes and change the IMEI/serial numbers with software which I hacked off the Internet. I started cloning bank websites, phishing for people's banking details to use online in various fraudulent transactions. There was even a time where the police were convinced that I was part of a huge syndicate, but much to their surprise, I was a one-man operation.

I was forever in trouble with the law, and as a result, I couldn't stay in one place for more than a year. My one track mind started deceiving me, and I was continuously lying to my wife about the reasons we had to move from house to house. Lying became part of my lifestyle. I was so addicted to pornography that I had to remind myself at times, that I have a beautiful wife at home who loves me unconditionally. I also loved her, but I loved porn more. I hated myself for neglecting my wife and children. I kept thinking of the times whereby we would go on family outings then I would be more concerned about whether the place where we were going to had internet access or not. Once we were driving back home to Johannesburg from Cape Town and I spent the full seventeen hours on the road chatting up another woman on my cell phone and staring at naked pictures of women with my wife sitting within an arm's length from me.

My cell phones were like body ligaments. I couldn't go anywhere without them. I always operated with two cell phones; one for business and one for my addiction which was permanently on vibrate as I didn't want my wife to know when I got calls or SMSs. I felt no shame and would pick unnecessary arguments with my wife just so that I could have an excuse to leave the house because being alone at home with my wife and children made me feel trapped. I treated my wife like dirt, in fact, lower than dirt. As long as my wife would stay at home, cook and clean and not bother me with the children's issues, then all would be okay. Other than that, I couldn't care less whether my wife had feelings or not. I spoke to her in any way I pleased. I was heartless and showed total disregard for my marriage vows.

According to Matthew 5:27, I had the trademark and the characteristics of an adulterer, because every woman I laid eyes upon, I would undress in my mind and long to sleep with. I lost total control of my life and gave myself over to my addiction, and I became a slave of Satan.

I want to tell everyone that if there is one addiction that surpasses all addictions, then it's pornography. Pornography is not just an addiction; it's a stronghold—a demonic force that controls your way of thinking. By the time I realized all this, my life was in complete disarray.

I look back at my life sixteen years later, and I see all the heartache and pain I caused in a lot of people's lives. I even committed the crime of bigamy by marrying another woman while being legally married, and today, that woman whom I deceived with open eyes has a child from me. A child I haven't met. So many times, after coming to my senses, I wanted to put a stop to it all and tell my wife everything, but I was too ashamed and couldn't build up the courage not to mention I was too afraid that my wife would leave me. However, little did I know it was the very wife whom I disrespected all these years who would forgive me when she told me that love keeps no record of wrongdoing according to 1 Corinthians 13.

All the lies, the deceit, everything just became too much for me to bear and I repeatedly called out to the Lord. Then the most dreadful thing happened: the SAPS were informed of my whereabouts, and I was arrested. I couldn't understand why because it now seemed that everything I was told about God was a lie. I was under the impression that if you call upon the Lord in your darkest hour, then the Lord will rescue you, but my wife reminded me that God does not listen to a sinner (John 9:31), but if I repent of my wicked ways, then He who is faithful and just will forgive me of my sins and cleanse me from all unrighteousness. Then I knew that the Lord had heard my cry, and suddenly, I understood the scriptures in Galatians 6:7 that what a man sows he shall also reap. I decided to take complete responsibility for my wrongdoings and stood up to face my giants.

I accepted Jesus as Lord of my life and prayed for God's will to be done in my life. I pleaded guilty in court to all charges against me. I will never forget my father-in-law's words to me the very first time I ended up in prison. He said that Christianity has a price tag attached to it, a price that Jesus already paid for me on the cross of Calvary.

I got sentenced that day, and I asked the Magistrate if I could comfort my wife who broke down in tears. I held my wife tight and asked her to be strong for me and for our children's sake as this was one journey I must take.

After my plea of guilt, I reminded myself every day that I did not choose God; God chose me. God's plan was always for me to prosper and never to harm me.

I came to learn the importance of walking in faith, for the Bible says that without faith, it is impossible to please God. My encouragement to every believer and non-believer is not to serve God for the benefits, but serve God in spirit and truth, for it is the reason we were created. Let your yes be yes and your no be no. Live at peace with one another and in everything, give praise unto God, be it in the good or bad times. I must tell you that Satan is still trying to remind me every day of my past, but God not only raised up a standard in me, He also renewed my mind according to Romans 12:2 and restored me by tasking the handcuffs off my soul and gave me back my life which the devil continuously robbed me of. Today, I can truly say that I am free from all the bondage including pornography because He whom the Son sets free is free indeed. Hallelujah.

I would like to send a stern warning to anyone who uses online chat programs like MXIT, Facebook, Twitter, WhatsApp, BBM, Google Chat and many more. One can be drawn easily into the web of social media. Remember, it is programs like these that ruin relationships and breaks up marriages.

To my darling wife, partner, and friend, I want to thank you for your love and support towards me during my time in incarceration. You have truly shown me the true meaning of love which as the word of God says, keeps no record of wrongdoing. I want to thank you for loving me past my mistakes and for submitting unto me despite the fact that I failed you so many times and in so many ways. I need you to know that it is because of your conduct that I came to know the Lord according to 1 Peter 3:1-2 and today, I want nothing else but to serve the Lord with you in spirit and trust. Babes, I love you with everything inside of me, from the deepest, abyss of my soul and heart. I know that I cannot change the past, but I am trusting God to raise a standard in our marriage and take us to greater heights in Christ Jesus.

To all my children, Dad is very proud of you. Even though Dad was not always there for you, Dad wants you to know that we can now be the family God intended us to be. A family fully numbered. Ohana means family, and family means no one gets left behind. Thank you for not leaving me behind.

From God-Hater and Mocker to Saved

Taylor, Surprise, AZ, USA

I knew Jesus was God at a young age and rejected Him in favor of a life of sin. I became addicted to video games and pornography for over twelve years.

I fluctuated between atheism and agnosticism. I made fun of Christians and thought they were just weak people with a crutch. I mocked God to people and made jokes about Him.

After years of depression and hating myself and hospitalizations for bipolar disorder, Jesus spoke to me. I was doing a very evil sin, and He told me in my heart to stop. I stopped and later smoked marijuana and was overwhelmed with feelings of remorse to my parents for all I'd done.

I took a shower after balling my eyes out to them, and my legs started to supernaturally wobble. I looked up and believed it was

Jesus Christ making this happen. I collapsed and said, "Jesus save me!" From then on, I dedicated my life to Him, and like they say, the rest is history.

I felt the dread and hopelessness inside me disappear and I felt clean. I've had wonderful moments of love with Jesus but also lots of dry periods.

I wish I could know how wonderful and perfect He is and worship Him all day. He's so wonderful. Never think you can out-sin His love because if you could, I'd be first on that list. He is my only joy and source of happiness.

I hope the people living in and loving sin who read this will please take my word for it—it's not worth it. I got everything I wanted in life in terms of sin and pleasure. None of it is worth hell or being without Jesus.

It was the Grace of God

Anonymous

I am from the eastern part of Nigeria, Onitsha. I used to live a life of complete sin. I stole from people, lied a lot, and I hated for no reason. I was a cultist. I used and dumped girls. I didn't go to church. I have even killed. I knew I was on the wrong side and knew I was doing the wrong thing.

I wanted to change, but I couldn't. I didn't even know how to pray. I wanted to share my problem, but I trusted nobody. I tried to leave the cult group but I couldn't because I was their leader. It was killing me, but I could do nothing about it.

On June 23, I was on my way to a friend's house to give him details about our operation in a bank, when a man came to me, gave me a paper and walked away. After some time had passed, I looked at the paper. It was an invitation to a church program titled, "GOD LOVES YOU, COME TO HIM." I laughed because it was funny to me. I told myself, "How can God love someone like me? As bad as I am?" When I showed my friend the paper, he told me that we should go. He would also like to know more about God's love.

On June 26, we went to the program, and during the praises, we couldn't say a word because we didn't know how to sing it. After the singing and prayers, it was time for the preaching. The man of God said something that made me want to change—his words moved me.

He said, "God loves you very much and He wants you to be His best friend. Why are you running away from Him? All His plans for you are good and not evil, and He is ready to forgive you of your sins, no matter the level of what you have done. He still wants you to be His friend." I was so moved and felt like something was going to explode in me.

After some time, the man of God said, "If you want to give your life to Christ, come out." I wanted to change, so I took the opportunity and came out of the seat, and he prayed for us. That moment, I felt like something was removed from me. It was my burden—my sins were lifted. I made my decision to change, and we were given a Bible.

When I got home, I studied the Bible and prayed. I stopped attending the cult meetings. I stopped all negativities in my life. I am still threatened by my former cult group, but I am happy to be a Christian; I am glad that I changed. I know I made the right choice. Life has not been easy for me, but I know things will get better with time. I am a proud Christian—praise God!

Freedom from Imprisonment

Romans 12:2

"And be not conformed to this world: but be ye transformed by the renewing of your mind, that ye may prove what is that good, and acceptable, and perfect, will of God."

King James Version

Face to Face with God in Solitary Confinement

Joshua Daniel Bligh, Vancouver, WA, USA

I was a staunch atheist for many years. I enjoyed reading the great skeptics like Richard Dawkins, Chris Hitchens, and Bertrand Russell. I thought, like all atheists ignorant of the experiential truth of Christ, that religion was the root of all the evil I saw in the world. I argued with Christians. I defiled a monument in Texas. I debated believers, including my mother, relishing my victories with self-adulation and a snickering disregard for their deepest held beliefs.

I had to go to prison for me to change. God more or less got me in a corner, against the ropes. His subtle beckoning had turned into a full-scale recovery effort. Here's my story:

In 2011, I went to prison for an assault. I was sentenced to five years (of which I served four). Things were going smoothly at first. I was housed at a minimum institution in Madras, Oregon.

I worked out in the community on a forestry crew and as a firefighter. I lived in a dorm setting. I slept and ate my meals at the prison, but otherwise, it didn't really feel like a prison.

I was eventually transferred to an unfenced, minimum custody forest camp in Tillamook. I went out to work four days a week planting trees and running chainsaw. The camp was small, and the food was good. We lived in twelve-man cabins. Things were going well. I was reading a lot of classic literature, thinking I was changing and becoming enlightened. Then God showed up.

One morning, when the crews were being called over the speakers to report to their respective forestry assignments, they told me I was being held in. I had nightmares all night and the night before. Around noon, I was called to Control. Two investigators were there. They told me to take a seat.

They said I was being indicted for very old criminal charges in another state. These charges, due to their circumstances, carried a five to ten-year prison sentence. My heart fell into my stomach. Not that I was guilty, per se, but I had seen how much help a public defender was in my assault case and I feared the result of having another one. It felt like my world imploded.

I had left two children out there without me. I hadn't seen them since I went to prison and their mother wasn't talking to me, wasn't even letting them receive my letters. I was already sorry to the point of self-hatred for having left them and coming to prison. I was sodden with remorse. Four years seemed like a marathon with no finish line. Now five more years? There was no way...

I was shackled and taken out of my pristine forest camp to a maximum facility—the penitentiary where I awaited paperwork on the charges. Meanwhile, I was adjusting not so well to the new, hardcore prison environment I found myself in. I got beat up over my wanting to retain my autonomy. I had to reset my two front teeth in my gums. The yard was bleak. There were big concrete walls, and gun towers. The walls, which were built in the late 19th century, told the tale of over a hundred and fifty years of misery and violence. Bullet holes scarred the walls.

I was beginning to fall into a deep depression. I traded my classic novels for books on astral projection and other occult practices. I got books of lucid dreaming and thought magic. I began my search for the infinite.

While I was at the penitentiary, I submitted my own paperwork, giving the offended state 180 days to come get me or drop the charges. This would put a fire under their butts to come get me, so I understood it. But I was wrong. An incident occurred where I had to be transported yet again to another medium/maximum security yard in Eastern Oregon, hundreds of miles from my family.

The paperwork was still in progress and the offended state was reviewing it. I was still under the delusion that the offended state had to drop the charges at the 180-day mark. It was now November. I had submitted the paperwork in May.

I met with a counselor who was dealing with the paperwork. During this meeting, she clarified the fact that the offended state does not have to come get me or drop the charges in 180 days. It's more of an informal courtesy, not a law.

I was already at a breaking point when I got this news. After I left her office, I could feel my soul literally being dragged around by my body like an anvil. I started to feel dizzy. I didn't want to go back to my cell. I had recently gotten a new cellmate who was a gang member; he was volatile and aggressive.

Instead of going back to my housing unit, I went to medical where I sat down in a chair and began to cry. I sobbed for more than an hour. I sobbed for my children who would have to be without their dad for another five to ten years if he survived. I sobbed because I had completely and utterly ruined my life. I broke down.

The nurse asked me if I was feeling suicidal. I told her yes. And I was escorted to solitary confinement on suicide watch.

I spent a total of ninety days in solitary confinement on 23-hour lock-down. At first, I loved it. It was a welcome break from all the nonsense that happens in general population. I sang to myself. I read books on dreaming. I kept a journal on scraps of paper. I ordered manuals on Buddhism and Thelema from the chapel library. I figured I'd learn how to meditate.

I practiced astral projection techniques with some success. I have reservations about sharing this subject as I feel that some might consider me a lunatic. But I figure that believers reading this are acquainted with the supernatural if they believe in the Immaculate Conception, the Resurrection, etc., so I will continue. During my astral projection experiments (self-induced out-of-body travel), I successfully pierced the veil. And it was terrifying. And I believe it opened the door for demonic attacks.

I was tormented by the guy in the cell over who would knock on the wall all day and all night. I am convinced a demonic spirit oppressed this individual. He would yell obscenities at other people all day through his cell door. He would decline his sleeping pills so he could stay awake all night knocking on the wall that separated us. It was mentally and emotionally challenging to be alone in a cell all day. I began to feel trapped for the first time when I became the object of his attacks. I finally retaliated, staying up all night and knocking my knuckles raw until he flooded his cell in order to be moved.

Time wore on in solitary. After he was moved, I got back into my routine of reading, writing, and meditating. It was the beginning of January when a thought came to my mind; a thought the likes of which hadn't come into my mind for a decade—to pick up a Bible. I'm sure now it was God putting it on my heart.

I fought it at first, but it kept on coming. *Pick up a Bible! Pick up a Bible!* So, when the book cart came around on its weekly trip past my cell, I grabbed the only Bible on the cart and opened it to Matthew.

I read most of Matthew, not without some tears in my eyes. When I reached the chapter about Jesus's prayer in the garden of Gethsemane, all defenses crumbled. I cried and cried. Jesus prayed: 'Father, take from me this cup of suffering.' This line lodged itself in my brain. Something that was simmering inside me came to a roiling boil.

I was heartbroken. Devastated. I felt hopeless. Hated. Guilty. Irredeemable. Abandoned. I felt like all my friends and family had turned their backs on me. Solitary confinement was merely an outward expression of an internal reality. For the first time in years, I dropped to my knees at the end of my bunk, and I prayed to God. I prayed the prayer that Jesus prayed in the garden. "Take away from me this cup of suffering," I told him, "and I will dedicate my life to you." I will live the rest of my life serving others. I prayed this prayer on the 21st of January, 2014. The morning afterward, I wrote it down in my scrap-paper journal.

The next day, January 22nd, a piece of mail arrived through the slot in my cell door. It was a letter from the public defender from the offended state. I trembled as I read the following words: "I have good news. The district attorney is thinking about dismissing the case. He doesn't feel it is worth it to bring you out here."

No words can express the way I felt in that cell. It was as if a breeze of electricity blew through my cell. I tingled all over; I shook with joy. I said, "Thank you, thank you, thank you!" Pointing to the ceiling of my cell; pointing to heaven.

God knew the lengths He had to go to recover me, and He took me there—the brink of complete physical, moral, and spiritual destitution. A place where everyone had turned their backs. He allowed it so that He could show me His face. He knew how deep my skepticism ran. He knew it would take a miracle this overt, this in my face. What a life it's been.

Since then, He has worked miracle after miracle in my life and the lives of my family members. A year after my deliverance, I was back at the forest camp in Tillamook fighting forest fires and preparing for my release, which happened on the 15th of November, 2015.

My last year in prison was punctuated with large doses of God's presence and tutoring. The Holy Spirit developed in me an insatiable appetite for God, the Bible, and fellowship. It's supernatural.

I played guitar in the Celebrate Recovery band and created a Christian comic book series for my children to help them cope with and understand my absence and the nature of incarceration. The comic was such a hit with them, and helped them so much, that I am currently adapting it to a more generalized format to reach other children of incarcerated parents. I am hoping for the best, as I am crowdfunding on Kickstarter right now for the resources to make this project a reality so we can distribute copies to inmates and their families free of charge.

I am currently in the beginning stages of rebuilding my life from the ground up by making the right decisions, being the dad I should have been. Balancing mandatory classes with finding work, plus finding time to write and draw can be tough. It is a process, and sometimes I find myself overheating from all the stimulus. But I think everything worthwhile is a process. My greatest wish is that God will use me and my story and skills to touch the lives of others, keeping true to my prayer—the contract that I made with God in that solitary confinement cell.

I know that Jesus's message is not about works, but grace. But a grateful heart wants to repay the kindness done to it. I want to serve God because of who He is, and what He has done for me, not what He could do.

I'll end this here. It has been a great relief getting this out of my system. I haven't had the chance yet to write about my prison experience in detail like this, and I feel a lot better now.
I'll end this testimony with a quote that sums up my experiences in prison:

"Some things are only found by the desperate."
- Bill Johnson, Pastor

Who am I? Now, I am a Son

William Austen

Who am I, Lord, that You love me, and have given Yourself for me?

My name is William Austen, and I have been so very deep in the world. All my life, I had mingled with this world which lies in wickedness. And I was certainly condemned with it.

The following is a shortened version of my life of who and what I was before I met Jesus, and how good God has been to me, and I'm sure He is and will be to whosoever calls upon His Name.

My childhood was plagued with many problems. My biological

father was a violent man. An alcoholic, a wife beater, and a drug addict. Fearing for her life, and that of her children, my mother decided to run from him. As soon as he knew our whereabouts, we would pack up and move. We were always on the run. My life as a child was filled with fear and insecurity.

By the time I attended high school, I was psychologically and emotionally damaged. I couldn't make friends. My grades were very low. I was always in trouble because of fighting and stealing. Most of my standard eight year, I was absent from school, hanging out with all the wrong kind of people—criminals.

In 1987, I was called up for two-year military service in the old South African defense force. I was sixteen at the time. It was a nightmare. It did me no good.

In 1997, I was sentenced to seven years imprisonment for fraud and theft. Life in jail was like being in hell. No freedom. No rights. Mental oppression. Gang wars. Murders. Rape. Corrupt prison officials. Loneliness. Fear. Lice. Dirty food. Diseases. Suicides. And my wife who I was married to at that time, divorced me and married my brother.

After spending four years in jail, I was released in May 2001. I had so many dreams; dreams of bonding with my son. Hopes of having a normal career; a normal life. But I quickly realized none of them were coming true. The baggage I was carrying from the past years made it all impossible. I was still the same man. Always in friendship with the greatest of sinners. I was again partaking in the worst of habits and lifestyles. I was often involved with drug dealers and gangsters.

As the years rushed by, I had become the most unstable person I have ever known. Madness, shame, hurt, anxiety, addiction, alcoholism, pornography, crime, depression, hatred, anger, revenge, broken heartedness, miserable, sadness, loneliness, violence, sickness, wickedness, godlessness, theft, paranoia, cruelty, betrayal, drug dealing, fighting, racism, imprisonment, gangster-ism, suicide- the fruits of being separated from God started manifesting.

I did not know, or rather I did not understand that the devil and his agents were warring against me. I did not know that their objective was to kill me and throw me into eternal misery! They very much succeeded. Six years had passed since I was released from prison. Suddenly, I found myself in a thousand pieces. I was a broken man. I was tired of crime. Tired of hurting people. Tired of life!

I had now come to the end of myself. There was just nothing left in me. Nothing! I sat alone in an empty room with a revolver stuck in my mouth. I know it sounds very weak of me, but what am I without the Lord as my strength? How terrible to be caught up in wickedness!

I didn't want to live anymore, but I was too afraid of dying. I was so scared of pulling the trigger. In my hour of need, as I sat all alone in my empty room, my life flashed before me. I cried out in desperation for Jesus to help me.

By the Mercy of our King, the Power of our Risen Savior, the Goodness of our Creator and by His Infinite Love and Compassion, after calling upon the Name above every other Name, the Name of Jesus Christ, God made me put that gun away and led me to a preacher who introduced me to Jesus Christ, the Messiah from Nazareth.

And then, Mercy rewrote my life. God allowed me to repent before Him of all my filthy sins and declared with my mouth, Jesus my Creator, King, and God. The Lord God Almighty touched me right there, and I was set free from the powers of darkness and every other thing that kept me in bondage. My chains were gone. Weeks later, I was baptized, and I have never been the same since then.

For the next two years, I was literally shouting from the rooftops what Jesus had done for me.

The desire in me was to give every drug addict, drug dealer, gangster, and every other broken person the same divine opportunity I had received, to meet Jesus, and to experience His healing power and life-changing mercies.

After two years of traveling the N1 highway, ministering in different towns, on the streets, in gang yards, in schools, and at jails, God led me to Mossel Bay. There I met Christa, who I am now married to. My lonely days had suddenly come to an end. My broken heart was finally mended. We have a son named Samuel. He was born on the 1st of April 2013. Both Christa and Samuel are a gift from God to me, and to this ministry.

I focus on one thing: Forgetting the past and looking forward to what lies ahead, I press on to reach the end of the race and receive the heavenly prize for which God, through Christ Jesus, is calling us. (Philippians 3:13,14)

Walking with Satan, now living with God!

Bill, Russell Springs, KY, USA

I'm thirty-nine years old and live in southern Kentucky. This is how my life was before becoming a servant of God.

I grew up in a broken home. Mom and Dad were always fighting. My mother, being a Jehovah's Witness, always tried to get me and my siblings to go with her on her nights of service.

I was sexually abused by the next door neighbor along with two other children. I was a child that struggled with many things in my younger years. My mother got remarried and got more active with the Jehovah's Witnesses.

When I turned nineteen, I graduated from high school and got married right after. I left for the Marine Corps in 1994.

While in boot camp, I witnessed the suicide of a Senior Drill instructor. I returned home later and decided to get into police work.

My desire to become a police officer at an early age became real in 1996. I started my journey when I was twenty-one years old. In 1998 while on duty, I was almost killed in the line of duty.

In 2000, I became dependent on pain medication (opiates) related to my prior injuries in 1998. I was the President of the local Fraternal Order of Police.

I was later investigated in 2003 for my use and ways of getting the drug of choice. The Attorney General's Office led the investigation. I pled guilty to criminal charges and was locked up for two and a half years. I fought for years to overcome the evilness of Satan.

In 2006, I got remarried and had a child with my current wife.

In 2009, I finally got clean and had remained clean to this very date. We relocated to a different area of Kentucky. I gave my life to the Lord and knew Jesus Christ is the Son of our God Almighty and died for our sins. I have served the Lord since and have never looked back. The Lord has blessed me in so many ways since serving Him. I have a child on the way by His Grace and Mercy!

I feel the calling from God to share my testimony far and wide to lead others to become saved and to serve our Creator! I believe we must give everything we have to the Lord and let Him control everything in our life. We have work to do for the Lord. I have the burning desire to travel anywhere to share what God can and will do if we just remain obedient to His Will! Praise the Lord, and do all things to glorify His name! Thanks for allowing me to render my testimony to give the Lord all the credit! God bless every soul on this earth!

Freedom from Bondage of Sin

Galatians 5:1

"Stand fast therefore in the liberty wherewith Christ hath made us free, and be not entangled again with the yoke of bondage."

King James Version

Feeling unfit for the presence of God

Anonymous, Arlington, WA, USA

I don't ever remember not believing in God or Jesus. When I was seven years old, Mom gathered my brothers and me together, (five, six, and seven), to tell us that we were Jews and that Jews don't believe that Jesus Christ is the Son of God. I can tell you that did not take hold on me at all and I never was taken by any of that.

At Christmas, we used to go to Dad's sister's family, who were Catholics and would sit on the sofa sometimes, just looking at the crucifix on the wall next to the hallway door. I would wonder about a lot of things like how it must have been to be crucified, and about His name, Christ; if that was His last name... but I never had any other thought, but that He was the Son of God.

As I got older, my brothers and I were very different in some ways, and we each had our own friends, but living in Southern California, it wouldn't be long before the uncleanness and evils that hold that place would eventually get to us. There was no religion in our house: Dad's family was originally Baptist but something happened, I think, and they all became Freemasons. I don't know if they tried to do this side by side, but I suspect that it was a conscious decision to not believe in every word of the Bible, and so they opened a very evil door and left the church altogether.

Mom's family is Jewish, of the priests, which as I came to understand later, after I was saved and started learning the Bible. That's what was probably behind the deep revolt and hostility to Jesus, which they apparently inherited. I can only think of a few, if that many, from the family, which are in any way open to the Lord and the Scriptures. In fact, some are outrageously hateful and hostile and blasphemous.

Well, to briefly tell my story of how I got saved, as I mentioned, I grew up in LA and Orange County, CA, during the end of the sixties and through the seventies. Needless to say, in a house with a determinedly non-religious environment, my brothers and I were vulnerable. Mom and Dad were good parents, as best they could, and had very tough times trying to get along and agree with each other on how we should be raised: this is the most common regret I hear from them today.

So, anyway, when I was about thirteen years old, I started having trouble with personal sins. By the time I was fifteen, I was into the "very cool" and "everybody's doing it" things, like drugs, rock music, and fornication. By the time I was seventeen, I got arrested for breaking and entering, and theft. So, I got to spend a few days in LA downtown Juvenile Hall. That was also about the time when I started learning the guitar and pretending that I wanted to be in a band. It never really happened the way my friends and I talked about and wished because none of us knew enough to get a job and earn money to buy the equipment.

Looking back now, I know it was God's mercy not to let me go that way with that kind of people. It was also in those days that I met several times, different ones who would "witness" Jesus and the Gospel to me. I was always open, agreeable, and cooperating with them, even saying the "sinner's prayer" if they wanted to lead me in it. I would go away afterward thinking about it, and wondering in the dark what it all meant.

At a certain point, a very close friend of mine, with whom I had thought we would form a great band one day, came to my house and was talking about Jesus and becoming a Christian. As he was my best friend, I went along agreeably with him, but after he left, I went back as usual to my "partying" ways and worthless friends. But this time, the Holy Spirit started convicting me of my sins, and that if I didn't quit them and get my life right with God, then I was heading to hell! It was so miserable! I could hardly function or maintain, and still, I just sat there like a lump, not repenting, not changing, not quitting what I was doing or the ungodly friends I was addicted to. I, even at one point, tried talking to some of them about the Lord and the Bible, and the intense hatred, hostility, and bullying insults were really kind of shocking: but still, I sat there!

Then one day, as a couple of those "friends" and me were driving around town under the influence (shall we say), and the rock music blaring as usual, all of a sudden, in a fraction of a moment, the music was silenced. I was completely straight and clear in my mind, and I heard a voice, in perfect English and perfect tone, saying to me, *"You are not fit for the presence of God!"* And just as suddenly, I heard the music playing again, and my friends in the front seat were still stoned. I was really shaken and scared and astonished. I said to them, "Did you hear that?" I got no response and could tell that they hadn't heard a thing. That was the moment, I think, when I determined to turn to God and really do what I was supposed to do, and repent and become a Christian.

By my luck, (the Lord's great mercy and guidance), my friend who had preached Jesus to me before came by just for a minute. I was happy to see him! Between, the first time he started talking about Jesus to me, he did come over once, but I really gave him a miserable time, quarreling and questioning the most idiotic nonsense about why I couldn't become a Christian. He ended up having to go after I gave him such a hard time. So, when I saw him when I needed him to help me to get right with the Lord, I was so glad to see him. I grabbed his arm and pulled him into the house. We went to my room, and I said to him, "What do I have to do to repent?" I repented and decided to follow Jesus.

Now, Jesus is everything to me, and I hope to finish my course with the unspeakable joy of finally seeing Him face to face, and worshiping at His feet. I'm so very grateful to the Lord for loving me, and not condemning me when He right could have.

Amazing Love

Elsia, Davao City, Philippines

I grew up in a Christian family. Christian in name, but without work and faith. Like in the word of God, faith without work is dead. Since high school, my life was very miserable, full of tribulations and I really searched out the love from others because I thought I could find happiness and love only in my friends.

I always joined dance contests with my friends. I got drunk every Saturday where my friends wanted to go. I joined Clan so that I could have lots of friends, and then on Sundays, I would go to church without passion because my mindset before in life was a normal life cycle to sleep, study, graduate, work, and to have family, then die, but I was wrong. I realized in the end that I really have a purpose as to why I live in this world. There, a friend asked me if I really wanted to have the true happiness and love? I said, "Yes, I want it, but how can I have it?" Then my friend prayed for me, and she got my number until such time she became my leader in a ministry.

I am really blessed by the word of God in John 3:16 & Jeremiah 29:11 and lots of verses that enlightened me. I cried because I thought nobody cared for me, nobody appreciated me, nobody loved me at all, but I was wrong. God does love me because He died for my sins and He shows His love there for me.

I thought I don't have a good future because of my wrong decisions but it's not; God has a bigger plan for me. I experienced the faithfulness of our God since I know Him well; I walked and gave my faith to Him no matter what happened as long as I do it to be with my Father God. Now, God blessed me with so much and gave the things that I'd never experienced before like I shared the faithfulness of God in me by sharing His Word with others. His love is amazing to me. I can't measure the love that God has given me; He never leaves me nor forsakes me, because He really does love me.

The love that I searched for, I found in God, the joy, love, and peace are in Him. All I need is in Him, and no one can give it to me except God. Now, I'm delighted and content with what God has done in my life, unlike before when I was without His guidance.

One thing I realized is that we cannot lean on our own understanding, but we need God in every decision that we make. Only God can satisfy us and no one else. I was blessed by God, and I know that someday, the transformation of my life will also happen to you. Each of us has a purpose and a future in God.

"Then spake Jesus again unto them, saying, I am the light of the world: he that followeth me shall not walk in darkness, but shall have the light of life." John 8:12 KJV

I Once Was Lost in a World of Sin

Anonymous

I know that God is real. All of my experiences remind me daily just how merciful and loving God really is. He turned my mess into a message, one I hope that can personally touch the hearts and lives of others.

I haven't always done the right thing, and most likely I have disappointed God at times. I know His grace is more than I can ever comprehend. If He can take my broken past and heal it then anything is possible with Him. What God intends to do with my life at this point I am not sure, but this I do know: I am not ashamed of Jesus. I put Him first and foremost.

I try to take it one day at a time, and try to focus on all the good things God has blessed me with rather than all the negatives like I had done my entire life before giving my life to Christ. I also know that in the Bible, it says:

"And we know that all things work together for good to them that love God, to them who are the called according to his purpose."
Romans 8:28 KJV

Once I was lost in a world of sin
My troubles did surround me to no end
I lived my life the way I chose
As the world passed my eyes were closed
To the ways of the world that surround us today
Never giving thanks or time to pray

My heart was cold and hard as stone
Until the day I gave my life
And threw away my heartache and strife

The day I accepted Jesus into my heart
Peace and happiness became a part
Of the feelings I felt deep inside
Where anger and loneliness did abide

Now I feel compelled to inform
I do not wish to feel forlorn
Instead to live my life anew
And tell others what Jesus can do

Accept him in your heart today
Because Jesus Christ is the only way
To live your life, with peace and love
That can only come from above
Let God rule over your life my friend
Not just this moment or today, but to the end.

The Author and Finisher of our Faith

Tony, Cashmore, Victoria, Australia

I was sitting outside by myself eating my lunch at work; my thoughts were on nothing in particular. I was startled by a voice as clear as if it had been someone sitting next to me.

"Tony, you need to get to know Me."

Did I just hear the voice of God? Who am I that God should talk to me?

Just then, my mate, Pete sat down next to me. I said to him, "You are probably going to think that I am mad but God just told me I need to get to know Him."

Expecting ridicule, Pete said, "That's great, mate. I'm a Christian, and I really need to get back to God too."

I thought, *this guy is taking the Mickey out of me.*

I said, "Are you playing with me?"

Pete said, "No, I really need to get back to God."

I asked him, "What's a Christian?" He replied, "A follower of Jesus!"

I gave it no more thought for several more months. I was going through a rough marriage and found out that my wife had a boyfriend. I took my rifle from the cupboard and loaded the ammunition, and I heard a prompting suggesting I go and see another friend of mine also, Peter. Isn't Jesus amazing? I haven't given my heart to the Lord, but He still loved me enough to talk to me!

I went to Peter's place. Peter was one of those crazy born-again people who believed that God talked to him! I told him to convince me why I shouldn't shoot my wife. He told me about Jesus and led me through the sinner's prayer. He said, "You are now a Christian."

I went out to my car. I didn't feel any different and thought that well, if that's being a Christian, I certainly don't know what has changed. I said, "God, if you really do love me, show me now!"

I was immediately filled with the Holy Spirit. I felt the most amazing unfathomable flooding of light. My anger was melted immediately, replaced with the uncontainable joy of knowing that God loves me! Wow! I could not wait to tell my wife and her boyfriend that I forgive them.

That was in 1989. I have professed my faith in Jesus, my Lord and Savior for twenty-seven years. Jesus is the author and finisher of our faith; salvation is from Him alone. It is a gift He gives us freely, nothing that we can do to gain favor with God. We were chosen before the foundation of the earth was laid. Jesus chose us! I praise God that He loved me enough to save me! I pray that this testimony encourages someone to open their heart to the voice of the Lord and allow Him to rescue you from eternity without Him, eternal damnation in hell!

෫ා

2 Timothy 1:8

"Be not thou therefore ashamed of the testimony of
our Lord, nor of me his prisoner: but be thou partaker
of the afflictions of the gospel
according to the power of God;"

King James Version

How to become a Christian
(a follower of Jesus Christ):

If you feel compelled to take your first step towards God, you can do that right now wherever you are.

1. Acknowledge the Problem: We have all sinned, and that sin separates us from God

No matter how good you think you are, no matter how many good things you try to do, it is still not good enough to get into heaven; it can't be earned but is a gift.

- "For all have sinned, and come short of the glory of God" Romans 3:23

- "For the wages of sin is death; but the gift of God is eternal life through Jesus Christ our Lord." Romans 6:23

- "And he said, That which cometh out of the man, that defileth the man. For from within, out of the heart of men, proceed evil thoughts, adulteries, fornications, murders, Thefts, covetousness, wickedness, deceit, lasciviousness, an evil eye, blasphemy, pride, foolishness; all these evil things come from within, and defile the man." Mark 7:20-23

2. Discover the Solution: Jesus

The only way for God to bridge the gap between Himself and us is through His Son, Jesus Christ. His death was a substitute for us; He paid the penalty for our sins.

- "For God so loved the world, that he gave his only begotten Son, that whosoever believeth in him should not perish, but have everlasting life." John 3:16

- "For Christ also hath once suffered for sins, the just for the unjust, that He might bring us to God." I Peter 3:18

- "Neither is there salvation in any other; for there is no other name under Heaven given among men, whereby we must be saved." Acts 4:12

3. Respond: Believe, Repent, Confess, Accept Jesus as the Lord and your Savior

To be saved, we must believe that Jesus is Lord and believe that He died for our sins. This confession acknowledges before God that we are unable to attain righteousness on our own and that we accept His plan for our lives.

- "...Believe on the Lord Jesus Christ, and thou shalt be saved..." Acts 16:31

- "Yet to all who receive him, to those who believed in his name, he gave the right to become children of God." John 1:12

- "Then Peter said unto them, Repent, and be baptized every one of you in the name of Jesus Christ for the remission of sins, and ye shall receive the gift of the Holy Ghost." Acts 2:38
- "I came not to call the righteous, but sinners to repentance" Luke 5:32

- "If we confess our sins, he is faithful and just to forgive us our sins and cleanse us from all unrighteousness." 1 John 1:9
- "That if thou shalt confess with thy mouth the Lord Jesus, and shalt believe in thine heart that God hath raised him from the dead, thou shalt be saved."
  Romans 10:9

Pray this prayer with sincerity of heart:

"Dear God, I believe in you and that your Son, Jesus Christ, is Lord. I believe in His sacrifice for my sins and His resurrection from the dead. I repent and ask forgiveness for my sins and I'm now deciding to follow you. Please, come into my life through the gift of your Holy Spirit. It is in the Lord Jesus' name that I ask and receive, Amen."

The Bible says doing these things with sincerity means you are a Christian (Christ follower) and will have eternal life in heaven. "These things have I written unto you that believe on the name of the Son of God; that ye may know that ye have eternal life, and that ye may believe on the name of the Son of God."
1 John 5:13

Use caution in trusting your feelings, as feelings change.
Stand on God's promises—they never change.

Recommended growth steps:

1. **Pray: you talk to God**

- "Praying always with all prayer and supplication in the Spirit, and watching thereunto with all perseverance and supplication for all saints;" Ephesians 6:8

- "I will therefore that men pray everywhere, lifting up holy hands, without wrath and doubting." 1 Timothy 2:8

- "Ask, and it shall be given you; seek, and ye shall find; knock, and it shall be opened unto you:" Matthew 7:7

2. **Read the Bible: God talks to you**

- "All scripture is given by inspiration of God, and is profitable for doctrine, for reproof, for correction, for instruction in righteousness:"
2 Timothy 3:16

3. **Join a church; encourage and support other Christians**

- "Not forsaking the assembling of ourselves together, as the manner of some is; but exhorting one another: and so much the more, as ye see the day approaching." Hebrews 10:25

- "Iron sharpeneth iron; so a man sharpeneth the countenance of his friend." Proverbs 27:17

4. **Share your faith in Christ with non-Christians**

- "And he said unto them, Go ye into all the world, and preach the gospel to every creature." Mark 16:15

5. **Worship God**

- John 4:24 "God is a Spirit: and they that worship him must worship him in spirit and in truth."

- Psalm 150:1-6 1 "Praise ye the LORD. Praise God in his sanctuary: praise him in the firmament of his power. Praise him for his mighty acts: praise him according to his excellent greatness. Praise him with the sound of the trumpet: praise him with the psaltery and harp. Praise him with the timbrel and dance: praise him with stringed instruments and organs. Praise him upon the loud cymbals: praise him upon the high sounding cymbals. Let every thing that hath breath praise the LORD. Praise ye the LORD."

6.   Be baptized

- "Go ye therefore, and teach all nations, baptizing them in the name of the Father, and of the Son, and of the Holy Ghost:"
  Matthew 28:19

7.   Take communion

- "For as often as ye eat this bread, and drink this cup, ye do shew the Lord's death till he come."
  1 Corinthians 11:26

8.   Strive to live a holy life

- Romans 12:2 – "And be not conformed to this world: but be ye transformed by the renewing of your mind, that ye may prove what [is] that good, and acceptable, and perfect, will of God."

- James 2:26 – "For as the body without the spirit is dead, so faith without works is dead also."

- John 8:11 - "...go, and sin no more."

Book and Publisher Information

Christian Testimonies
Published by Pure Truth Publications

Pure Truth Publications™
1000 N Green Valley Pkwy #440-210
Henderson, NV 89074
www.PureTruthPublications.com

Proceeds help support the King James Bible Online to help spread
the Word online.

May God bless you!

Special Offers

We hope you have enjoyed this Christian Testimonies book and we would love to hear your feedback!

If you have a minute to share your input on these 4 questions, we would greatly appreciate it. Simply type the following URL into your computer or mobile device's web browser:

https://goo.gl/gE9Js4

You will receive a complimentary ebook after 4 brief questions.

Save 10% on King James Bibles

For those looking for physical King James Bibles (including those in giant print), they are available at either URL below. Enter the following coupon code at checkout to save 10%: *SURVEY10*

https://www.kingjamesbibleonline.org/King-James-Bible-Store/

Made in the USA
Middletown, DE
16 March 2023

26882022R00070